Copyright © 2023 by Jilesh Thilakan

All rights reserved. No part of this book may be reproduced, distributed, or transmitted in any form or by any means, including photocopying, recording, or other electronic or mechanical methods, without the prior written permission of the copyright holder, except in the case of brief quotations embodied in critical reviews and certain other non-commercial uses permitted by copyright law.
For permissions requests, write to the publisher at the address below:
Publisher: Jilesh Thilakan, India
Website: www.healingoraclewisdom.com[1]
Email: drjilesht@gmail.com
Cover design by Jilesh Thilakan

Disclaimer: The information provided in this book is for general informational purposes only. The content is based on the concept of spiritual psychosis and finding clarity. The reader understands and acknowledges that spiritual psychosis is a complex and sensitive topic. This book is not intended as a substitute for professional medical or psychological advice. It is important to consult with qualified healthcare professionals or mental health experts if you suspect or experience symptoms related to spiritual psychosis.

The author and publisher disclaim any liability for any loss or damage incurred by the reader or any third party directly or indirectly as a result of the use or application of the information presented in this book. It is the responsibility of the reader to exercise personal

---

1. https://www.healingoraclewisdom.com/

discernment and seek appropriate professional guidance when dealing with matters related to mental health and spiritual experiences.

The book aims to provide insights and perspectives on spiritual psychosis and finding clarity. However, individual experiences may vary, and it is important to approach this subject matter with caution and respect for one's own well-being.

About the Author

Dr. Jilesh is a renowned and highly rated Spiritual healer, manifestation expert, spell caster, psychotherapist, life coach, and master of business administration. With extensive experience and expertise in the field, Dr. Jilesh has garnered a reputation as a trusted authority in the realm of manifestation and personal transformation.

As a highly rated manifestation expert and spell caster on Fiverr, Check Global Reviews here - https://www.fiverr.com/jileshthilakan?up_rollout=true[1] Dr.Jilesh has assisted countless individuals in manifesting their desires and achieving their goals. Through his deep understanding of the principles of manifestation, Dr. Jilesh has helped clients tap into their innate power to create their dream reality.

In addition to his work on Fiverr, **Dr. Jilesh has also excelled as a highly rated instructor on Udemy, with more than 30k students** Check his personal development courses here - https://www.udemy.com/user/jilesh-thilakan/ [2] sharing his knowledge and empowering students worldwide to harness the power of manifestation. With a passion for teaching and a commitment to providing valuable insights, Dr. Jilesh has garnered a loyal following of students who have experienced transformation and success under his guidance.

Dr. Jilesh's expertise extends beyond manifestation, as he is also a qualified psychotherapist and life coach. His background in psychology and counselling allows him to provide holistic support to individuals seeking personal growth and transformation. Through his empathetic approach and profound insights, Dr. Jilesh helps clients overcome challenges, break through limiting beliefs, and create lasting positive change in their lives.

Furthermore, Dr. Jilesh holds a master's degree in business administration, which adds a unique perspective to his work. His understanding of business principles and strategies allows him to guide individuals in aligning their personal goals with professional success, creating a harmonious balance between their aspirations and career pursuits.

With a diverse skill set and a genuine passion for helping others, Dr. Jilesh is committed to empowering individuals to unlock their full potential and manifest a life of abundance, fulfilment, and joy. Through his teachings, guidance, and transformative techniques, he aims to inspire and support others on their journey towards manifesting their deepest desires and living their best lives. **For more about Author checkout his Blog-** https://www.healingoraclewisdom.com/

---

1. https://www.fiverr.com/jileshthilakan?up_rollout=true
2. https://www.udemy.com/user/jilesh-thilakan/

Introduction

SPIRITUAL PSYCHOSIS: A GUIDE TO SPIRITUAL PSYCHOSIS FOR FINDING CLARITY

Beyond the boundaries of our everyday reality lies a realm shrouded in mystery and profound awakening - the realm of spirituality. It is a realm that beckons the seekers, the ones yearning to unearth the depths of their souls and discover a profound clarity that transcends the mundane. Yet, hidden amidst the ethereal beauty of this spiritual path lies a phenomenon that defies comprehension: spiritual psychosis.

In "A Guide to Spiritual Psychosis for Finding Clarity," we embark on an extraordinary journey - a journey that unveils the enigmatic shadows and illuminates the transformative power that lies within this unexplored terrain. Prepare to embark on an exploration that will challenge your preconceptions, ignite your curiosity, and expand the boundaries of your understanding.

Within these pages, you will encounter stories of souls teetering on the precipice between spiritual awakening and psychological disturbance. You will delve into the depths of their struggles, their triumphs, and the delicate dance between chaos and clarity. Prepare to witness the unravelling of the intricate tapestry that weaves spirituality and psychological well-being together, as we navigate the treacherous labyrinth of spiritual psychosis.

But fear not, dear reader, for this guide is not meant to frighten or discourage. Rather, it serves as a torch-bearer through the darkest corners of the spiritual journey, providing insights, tools, and guidance to navigate the complexities of spiritual psychosis. Here, you will find a roadmap to reclaim your inner clarity - a clarity that transcends the confusion and leads to profound enlightenment.

With each turn of the page, you will be introduced to transformative practices, ancient wisdom, and modern methodologies, all carefully crafted to illuminate the shadows that threaten to engulf the path. Discover techniques for grounding the self, integrating spirituality with psychology, and embracing the delicate balance between the spiritual and the mundane. Engage in introspective exercises, harness the power of mindfulness, and tap into the boundless potential of your consciousness.

Prepare to embark on a transformative odyssey - an odyssey that will challenge your perceptions, ignite your inner fire, and ultimately guide you toward the radiant light of clarity. "A Guide to Spiritual Psychosis for Finding Clarity" invites you to embark on a profound exploration—one that will forever change your perception of spirituality, psychology, and the limitless potential of the human spirit.

Open your heart, still your mind, and let the journey begin. The answers await those brave enough to step into the mystical realm of spiritual psychosis. Are you ready to unlock the door and discover the boundless clarity that lies beyond?

Chapter 1
The Calling of the Soul

The Whispers of the Soul

Deep within the vast landscape of our being, a gentle voice whispers - a voice that emanates from the depths of our soul. It is a voice that calls to us, beckoning us to embark on a profound journey of self-discovery, transformation, and spiritual growth. These whispers of the soul carry with them a profound longing for connection, purpose, and authenticity - a yearning that often emerges as a quiet ache in the depths of our being. The whispers of the soul are not loud and demanding; they are subtle, soft, and easily drowned out by the noise of everyday life. Yet, they persist, persistently nudging us to pay attention and heed their call. These whispers manifest in various ways - an intuitive hunch, a recurring thought, a deep longing, or a sense of restlessness. They may come to us in dreams, through encounters with synchronicities, or in moments of deep introspection. They are the subtle threads that weave through the fabric of our existence, guiding us towards a deeper understanding of ourselves and our place in the world. As we learn to attune ourselves to these whispers, we begin to unravel the layers of conditioning, societal expectations, and fear that have clouded our clarity. We recognize that these whispers are the voice of our authentic self, seeking to guide us back to a state of alignment and wholeness. They carry the wisdom of our true nature, gently reminding us of our inherent worth and the unique gifts we bring to the world. To truly hear and honour the whispers of the soul, we must create space for deep listening and reflection. This may involve carving out moments of stillness in our busy lives, retreating into nature, or engaging in practices such as meditation or contemplation. In these moments of quietude, we open ourselves to the vast expanse of our inner landscape, allowing the whispers to rise to the surface of our consciousness.

As we listen, we may encounter resistance - a fear of the unknown, doubts, or limiting beliefs that have kept us tethered to a state of complacency or mediocrity. Yet, as we embrace the whispers, we find the courage to step into the unknown, to explore the uncharted territories of our being. We recognize that the path to clarity and self-discovery may be filled with uncertainty, but it is through this uncertainty that growth and transformation emerge. The whispers of the soul are not external directives or prescriptive instructions; they are invitations - an invitation to embark on a journey of self-discovery, to dive into the depths of our being, and to uncover the hidden treasures that lie within. They invite us to question, to explore, and to seek answers beyond the superficial layers of existence. They beckon us towards a life of authenticity,

purpose, and profound connection with our true selves and the world around us.

As we learn to embrace and honour the whispers of the soul, we open ourselves to the transformative power of self-discovery. We begin to unravel the narratives that have shaped our lives, challenging the beliefs and patterns that no longer serve our growth and well-being. We forge a deep and intimate relationship with ourselves, cultivating self-compassion, self-acceptance, and self-love. In this sacred dance with the whispers of the soul, we come to recognize that the longing within us is not a burden but a gift - a compass that guides us towards a life of greater clarity, purpose, and authenticity. As we embark on this journey, we are invited to trust the wisdom that resides within and to surrender to the unfolding of our own unique path. May you find the courage to listen to the whispers of your soul, to honour the call that stirs within you, and to embark on a transformative journey of self-discovery. May you find solace, guidance, and profound clarity as you attune yourself to the wisdom that emanates from the depths of your being. Embrace the whispers, for they hold the keys to unlocking the profound depths of your true essence and the limitless possibilities that await you on this sacred journey of the soul.

Awakening to the Call

In the tapestry of our lives, there comes a time when we begin to feel a stirring - a subtle shift in our awareness, an inner longing that calls us to awaken to something greater. This section explores the profound experience of awakening to the call of the soul and the transformative journey that unfolds as we respond to its beckoning. The awakening to the call often emerges as a result of a deep yearning - a yearning for meaning, purpose, and a connection that transcends the boundaries of the material world. It may come to us during moments of introspection, when we find ourselves questioning the status quo, or in times of immense change or personal crisis. These pivotal moments invite us to look beyond the surface-level existence and search for answers that reside in the depths of our being. As we begin to awaken, we start to notice synchronicities - seemingly coincidental events that hold profound significance. These synchronicities act as gentle nudges from the universe, guiding us towards our true path. They may manifest as encounters with like-minded individuals, the sudden appearance of books, quotes, or teachings that resonate deeply, or a series of serendipitous events that leave us in awe of the interconnectedness of life.

With each synchronicity, the whispers of the soul grow louder, and our awareness expands. We become attuned to the subtle signs and symbols that

litter our path, recognizing them as guideposts leading us towards our authentic selves. The call of the soul becomes undeniable - a persistent presence that cannot be ignored. As we awaken to the call, we embark on a transformative journey of self-discovery. We step out of the confines of societal expectations and venture into uncharted territory, guided by the wisdom that emanates from within. It is a journey of shedding old identities and beliefs, of questioning the constructs that have shaped our lives, and of exploring the vast depths of our being.

This journey may not be without its challenges. We may encounter resistance -both from within ourselves and from external sources. Doubts may arise, fuelled by societal norms or the fear of the unknown. Yet, in these moments of doubt, we are invited to trust in the process, to lean into the wisdom that emanates from the core of our being. As we respond to the call, we cultivate resilience and inner strength. We learn to navigate the challenges with grace and humility, recognizing that each obstacle is an opportunity for growth and self-discovery. We embrace the lessons that arise, knowing that they hold the keys to unlocking our true potential and expanding our awareness. Awakening to the call is not a one-time event; it is a continuous process of deepening our connection with our authentic selves and the world around us. It is a lifelong journey of self-discovery, unfolding in its own unique rhythm. With each step we take, we uncover new layers of insight, wisdom, and clarity, gaining a deeper understanding of our purpose and the intricate tapestry of existence. As we fully embrace the awakening, we become active participants in our own transformation. We cultivate a deep sense of presence and mindfulness, recognizing that the call of the soul is not separate from our everyday lives but an intrinsic part of it. We integrate the wisdom gained from the awakening into our relationships, our work, and our interactions with the world.

In conclusion, the awakening to the call of the soul is a profound and transformative experience. It invites us to transcend the limitations of the mundane and embark on a journey of self-discovery, purpose, and profound connection. As we respond to this call, we step into our true power, embracing the vast potential that resides within us. May you embrace the awakening with an open heart, listen to the whispers of your soul, and embark on a journey of self-discovery and growth. May you find clarity, purpose, and profound fulfilment as you navigate the path that unfolds before you.

The Journey of Self-Discovery

Within the depths of our being lies a vast and unexplored landscape - a terrain rich with hidden treasures, profound insights, and the potential for deep transformation. This section delves into the significance of embarking on the journey of self-discovery, the transformative power it holds, and the clarity that emerges as we unravel the layers of our existence. The journey of self-discovery is a sacred quest - an inward exploration that takes us beyond the surface-level understanding of ourselves and into the realms of our authentic essence. It is an invitation to delve into the recesses of our being, to question, to reflect, and to unveil the truths that have been obscured by the noise of everyday life. As we embark on this journey, we enter into a state of self-reflection and introspection. We carve out sacred moments of stillness amidst the busyness of our lives, creating space for deep listening and contemplation. In these moments, we invite the whispers of our soul to rise to the surface, allowing them to guide us towards a deeper understanding of who we truly are.

The journey of self-discovery is not a linear path, nor does it have a predetermined destination. It is a continual process of exploration, unfolding in its own unique rhythm. It involves embracing the complexities of our being - the light and the shadow, the strengths and the vulnerabilities, the triumphs and the wounds.

As we navigate this journey, we encounter aspects of ourselves that have been hidden, forgotten, or denied. We shine the light of awareness upon these aspects, bringing them into conscious awareness. In doing so, we begin to integrate these fragmented parts, healing the wounds and releasing the limitations that have hindered our growth. The journey of self-discovery invites us to question the narratives that have shaped our lives - the beliefs, expectations, and conditioning that have influenced our choices and perceptions. We challenge the notions of who we think we are, unravelling the layers of identities that have been constructed over time. Through this process of questioning and unravelling, we gain a deeper understanding of our authentic

essence - the core of our being that transcends societal roles, expectations, and external validations.

As we navigate the journey, we uncover our passions, our values, and the unique gifts we bring to the world. We recognize the patterns and tendencies that shape our thoughts, emotions, and actions, and we cultivate a deeper sense of self-awareness. This self-awareness becomes a compass, guiding us towards a life of alignment and authenticity. The journey of self-discovery is not without

its challenges. We may encounter resistance - internal and external forces that attempt to keep us stagnant or conforming to societal norms. Doubts may arise, and fears may surface. Yet, it is in the face of these challenges that we cultivate resilience, courage, and a deep trust in the process. Throughout the journey, we uncover insights, wisdom, and profound moments of clarity. We come to recognize that self-discovery is not merely an intellectual exercise but a deeply embodied experience - a merging of the mind, body, and spirit. We engage in practices that foster our well-being, such as meditation, yoga, creative expression, or time spent in nature. These practices become anchors, grounding us in the present moment and deepening our connection with our inner selves. As the journey unfolds, we find ourselves in a state of constant evolution - a continual shedding of old layers and a rebirth of our authentic essence. We cultivate a deep sense of self-acceptance and compassion, honouring every aspect of our being with love and understanding.

In conclusion, the journey of self-discovery is a profound and transformative odyssey. It invites us to explore the depths of our being, to unravel the layers of conditioning, and to embrace the fullness of our authentic essence. As we embark on this sacred quest, we gain clarity, purpose, and a deep connection with our true selves. May you embark on the journey of self-discovery with an open heart and a curious mind, embracing the transformative power that resides within you. May you uncover the hidden treasures that lie within, forging a deep and intimate relationship with your true essence. Embrace the journey, for it holds the key to profound clarity, growth, and a life lived in alignment with your soul's purpose.

Navigating the Challenges

The journey of self-discovery is not without its challenges. As we navigate the depths of our being, we encounter obstacles, doubts, and resistance that can

hinder our progress. This section explores the significance of navigating these challenges with resilience, grace, and a deep trust in the transformative process.

One of the primary challenges we may encounter on the journey is the resistance that arises within ourselves. It is natural for the ego to cling to familiar patterns and identities, even if they no longer serve our growth and well-being. The ego fears the unknown, and it may attempt to keep us within the confines of our comfort zones. However, it is through recognizing and embracing this resistance that we open ourselves to the transformative power of

self-discovery. We learn to navigate the internal resistance by cultivating self-compassion and self-acceptance. We acknowledge that resistance is a normal part of the journey and that it arises as a protective mechanism. By extending kindness and understanding towards ourselves, we create a safe space to explore the edges of our comfort zones and to transcend the limitations that hold us back. External challenges may also arise as we embark on the journey of self-discovery. The people, environments, or systems around us may resist our growth, projecting their own fears and insecurities onto our transformative process. We may face criticism, judgment, or a lack of understanding from those who do not resonate with our path. Navigating these external challenges requires us to maintain a strong sense of inner conviction and to set healthy boundaries. We honour our own truth and prioritize our well-being, knowing that our journey of self-discovery is unique to us. We surround ourselves with supportive individuals who uplift and encourage our growth, seeking out communities and resources that align with our values and aspirations.

Doubts and insecurities may also arise along the journey. We may question our abilities, our worthiness, or the validity of our own experiences. These doubts can undermine our clarity and deter us from fully embracing our authentic essence. However, it is through confronting these doubts with self-compassion and self-reflection that we transcend them. We learn to cultivate a sense of inner trust - an unwavering belief in our own inherent wisdom and the transformative power of the journey. We draw strength from the insights and moments of clarity we have experienced, using them as beacons of guidance during times of uncertainty. We remind ourselves that the doubts and insecurities are temporary and that they do not define us or our path. The journey of self-discovery may also bring us face to face with our own shadows - the aspects of ourselves that we have suppressed or disowned. These shadows hold the wounds, fears, and unresolved emotions that can hinder our growth and clarity. However, it is through embracing these shadows with compassion and courage that we facilitate profound healing and transformation.

We engage in shadow work, delving into the depths of our being with curiosity and a willingness to explore the darker corners of our psyche. Through practices such as journaling, therapy, or energy healing, we bring awareness to the shadows and shed light upon them. In doing so, we integrate and heal these aspects, allowing for a greater sense of wholeness and clarity to emerge.

As we navigate the challenges on the journey of self-discovery, we learn the art of surrender. We recognize that not everything is within our control and that the transformative process has its own divine timing.

We surrender to the unfolding of the journey, trusting that each challenge is an opportunity for growth and that clarity will emerge in its own time.

In conclusion, navigating the challenges on the journey of self-discovery is an integral part of the transformative process. By recognizing and embracing resistance, setting healthy boundaries, confronting doubts and insecurities, and embracing our shadows with compassion, we cultivate resilience and trust in the transformative power of self-discovery. May you navigate these challenges with grace and perseverance, knowing that each hurdle is an invitation for growth and profound clarity. Embrace the challenges, for they are the stepping stones that lead you towards a life of authenticity, purpose, and profound self-understanding.

Embracing the Unfolding

The journey of self-discovery is a dynamic and ever-evolving process. It unfolds in its own unique rhythm, guiding us towards greater clarity, growth, and self-understanding. This section explores the significance of embracing the unfolding nature of the journey and the transformative power that emerges when we surrender to its wisdom. Embracing the unfolding requires us to release our attachments to specific outcomes or timelines. It invites us to relinquish the need for control and to trust in the divine intelligence that orchestrates our journey. As we surrender to the natural flow of the process, we open ourselves to the vast potential and opportunities that lie beyond our limited perceptions. The unfolding of the journey may not always align with our expectations or desires. We may encounter detours, unexpected challenges, or periods of uncertainty. However, it is in these moments that we are invited to deepen our trust and embrace the wisdom that arises from the unknown. We learn to cultivate patience and resilience, knowing that growth and transformation take time. We recognize that the journey is not a linear path but a spiral, revisiting themes and lessons as we ascend to new levels of understanding. Through each twist and turn, we gain deeper insights, uncover hidden aspects of ourselves, and expand our capacity for clarity and self-awareness.

Embracing the unfolding also involves being fully present in the here and now. It is through anchoring ourselves in the present moment that we access the richness and depth of our experiences. We learn to appreciate the beauty and lessons that emerge in each step of the journey, regardless of whether they align with our preconceived notions of success or progress.

We engage in practices that cultivate presence, such as mindfulness, meditation, or conscious breathing. These practices ground us in the present moment, allowing us to fully immerse ourselves in the richness of our inner and outer landscapes. By embracing the unfolding with a sense of presence, we heighten our receptivity to the insights, synchronicities, and opportunities that arise along the way. As we surrender to the unfolding, we attune ourselves to the guidance of our intuition and the wisdom of the universe. We learn to listen to the whispers of our soul and to trust the inner compass that navigates us through the intricacies of the journey. We recognize that the journey itself is a teacher—an ever-present source of wisdom and growth. Embracing the unfolding also involves re framing our perspective on challenges and setbacks. We shift from viewing them as obstacles to recognizing them as opportunities for growth and self-discovery. We understand that even in the face of adversity, clarity and transformation can emerge. We learn to embrace the lessons inherent in each challenge and to use them as catalysts for our evolution.

Throughout the journey, we remain open to the possibility of surprises, miracles, and serendipitous encounters. We allow ourselves to be guided by the currents of synchronicity, recognizing that the universe conspires to support our growth and expansion. Embracing the unfolding means being receptive to the signs, symbols, and opportunities that present themselves, knowing that they are guiding us towards greater clarity and alignment.

In conclusion, embracing the unfolding of the journey of self-discovery is an essential aspect of the transformative process. By surrendering to the divine timing, releasing attachments, and cultivating presence, we open ourselves to the profound wisdom and transformative power that emerge along the way. May you embrace the unfolding with an open heart and a sense of trust, knowing that each step of the journey holds the potential for clarity, growth, and self-understanding. Embrace the unfolding, for it is through this surrender that you align with the inherent wisdom and infinite possibilities that reside within you.

Chapter 2
Unveiling the Shadows

Recognizing the Shadows

Within the depths of our being, hidden beneath the surface of our conscious awareness, lie the shadows - the aspects of ourselves that we have suppressed, denied, or disowned. To embark on the journey of self-discovery, we must first acknowledge the existence of the shadows within us. These shadows are formed by our past experiences, traumas, conditioning, and the parts of ourselves that we deem unworthy or unacceptable. They represent the unhealed wounds and unresolved emotions that have been buried in the recesses of our subconscious.

Recognizing the shadows requires a willingness to confront the parts of ourselves that we have been reluctant to acknowledge. It involves embracing vulnerability and embracing the discomfort that arises when we face aspects of ourselves that we may have long ignored or denied. By shining the light of awareness upon these shadows, we initiate the process of healing and transformation.

Embracing the Shadow Work

Embracing the shadows is an act of self-compassion and self-acceptance. It is a courageous commitment to face the parts of ourselves that we may have judged or rejected. We cultivate a sense of curiosity and non-judgment as we delve into the depths of our shadows. Through practices such as journaling, therapy, meditation, or creative expression, we invite the shadows to come forth, giving them a voice and allowing their wisdom to be revealed.

As we engage in shadow work, we gain insights into the underlying beliefs, patterns, and behaviours that have shaped our lives. We develop a deeper understanding of how these shadows have influenced our relationships, choices, and overall well-being. Through this process, we come to recognize that the shadows are not to be feared or rejected, but to be embraced as integral aspects of our wholeness.

Healing and Integration

Healing and integration are integral aspects of the shadow work process. Once we have recognized and embraced our shadows, we embark on a journey of

healing and integration, bringing these aspects back into the wholeness of our being. Healing the shadows involves extending compassion and forgiveness towards ourselves. We release the judgments and self-criticism that have kept us locked in patterns of shame or guilt. We allow ourselves to feel the emotions that arise, acknowledging them as valuable messengers of our healing process.

Through practices such as self-care, self-compassion, and energy healing, we facilitate the release of old wounds and cultivate a state of emotional well-being. Integration occurs when we fully embrace and integrate the lessons and gifts that our shadows offer. We recognize that the shadows hold valuable insights and wisdom that can enhance our personal growth and transformation. By integrating the shadows, we gain a greater understanding of our true essence and the multifaceted nature of our being.

Transcending the Shadows

As we engage in the journey of self-discovery and shadow work, we gradually transcend the shadows. We rise above the limitations and conditioning that have kept us confined, allowing our true essence to shine forth. We reclaim the disowned aspects of ourselves and integrate them into our identity, celebrating the fullness of our being. We no longer allow the shadows to dictate our choices or define our self-worth. Instead, we cultivate a deep sense of self-acceptance and self-love, embracing the wholeness that emerges from the integration of all aspects of ourselves. As we transcend the shadows, we free ourselves from the limitations and patterns that have held us back. We gain clarity, authenticity, and a deeper connection with our true essence. We embody our newfound wisdom and live from a place of empowerment, inspiring others to embrace their own shadows and embark on their own journeys of self-discovery.

In conclusion, the journey of unveiling the shadows is a transformative process that invites us to recognize, embrace, and integrate the hidden aspects of our being. By engaging in shadow work, healing, and integration, we transcend the limitations that have kept us confined and emerge into a state of wholeness and

authenticity. May you embark on this journey with courage and compassion, knowing that the shadows hold the keys to profound self-understanding and liberation. Embrace the shadows, for they are the gateways to your deepest wisdom and the transformative power that resides within you.

Chapter 3
The Inner Alchemy

Understanding the Alchemical Process

Within the depths of our being lies the potential for profound transformation and spiritual evolution.. Inner alchemy is an ancient and mystical practice that seeks to transmute the lead of our lower aspects into the gold of our highest potential. It is a process of purification, refinement, and integration, where we harness the transformative power of our inner fire to transmute and elevate our consciousness. The alchemical process begins with the stage of nigredo, the dark night of the soul - a period of dissolution, introspection, and confronting our shadows. It is a time of deep inner work, where we face the challenges and limitations that have held us back. We confront the leaden aspects of our being, allowing them to be transformed by the fires of awareness and self-reflection.

Dissolving the Ego

The ego, with its attachments, identifications, and patterns, often hinders our growth and keeps us confined within limited perspectives. Through the process of dissolution, we release the grip of the ego and open ourselves to a higher state of consciousness.

Dissolving the ego involves a profound surrender - a letting go of the identities and attachments that no longer serve our growth. We recognize the illusory nature of the ego and its tendency to create separation and suffering. Through practices such as meditation, self-inquiry, and self-reflection, we cultivate a state of witnessing awareness, allowing the ego to dissolve into the vast expanse of our true nature.

Awakening the Divine Spark

The inner alchemical process also involves awakening the divine spark within us - the dormant aspect of our being that holds infinite potential and connection to the divine. Awakening the divine spark requires a shift in consciousness - an expansion of our awareness beyond the limitations of the personal self. We cultivate a deep sense of presence, opening ourselves to the divine intelligence that permeates all of creation. Through practices such as meditation, prayer, or sacred rituals, we invite the divine to flow through us, awakening our innate wisdom, love, and creative potential.

Integration and Transmutation

Integration and transmutation are integral aspects of the inner alchemical process. As we dissolve the ego and awaken the divine spark, we enter a stage of integration - bringing together the fragmented aspects of our being into a unified whole. Through integration, we bridge the gap between the spiritual and the mundane, living in alignment with our true essence. Transmutation is the alchemical process of transforming the base elements of our being into higher states of consciousness and spiritual realization. It is through the fires of transmutation that we release old patterns, conditioning, and limitations, allowing our true essence to shine forth. Through practices such as self-reflection, meditation, or energy healing, we facilitate the transmutation of lower vibrations into higher frequencies, aligning ourselves with our soul's purpose and divine potential.

Embodying the Philosopher's Stone

The culmination of the inner alchemical process is the embodiment of the philosopher's stone - the symbol of enlightenment, wholeness, and the integration of all aspects of our being. Embodying the philosopher's stone involves living from a state of deep presence, love, and wisdom. It is a state of unity consciousness, where we recognize the interconnectedness of all beings and the divinity that resides within us and all of creation. Through this embodiment, we become vessels of transformation, radiating the transformative power of our true essence into the world.

In conclusion, the journey of inner alchemy is a profound and transformative process that leads us to the embodiment of our highest potential. By understanding and engaging in the stages and principles of the alchemical process - dissolution, awakening, integration, and transmutation - we cultivate a deep connection with our true nature and align with the divine spark within us. May you embrace the inner alchemical process with curiosity and dedication, knowing that within you lies the potential for profound transformation, spiritual evolution, and the embodiment of your highest self. Embrace the journey of inner alchemy, for it holds the keys to unlocking the infinite potential that resides within you.

Chapter 4
Finding Balance in Chaos

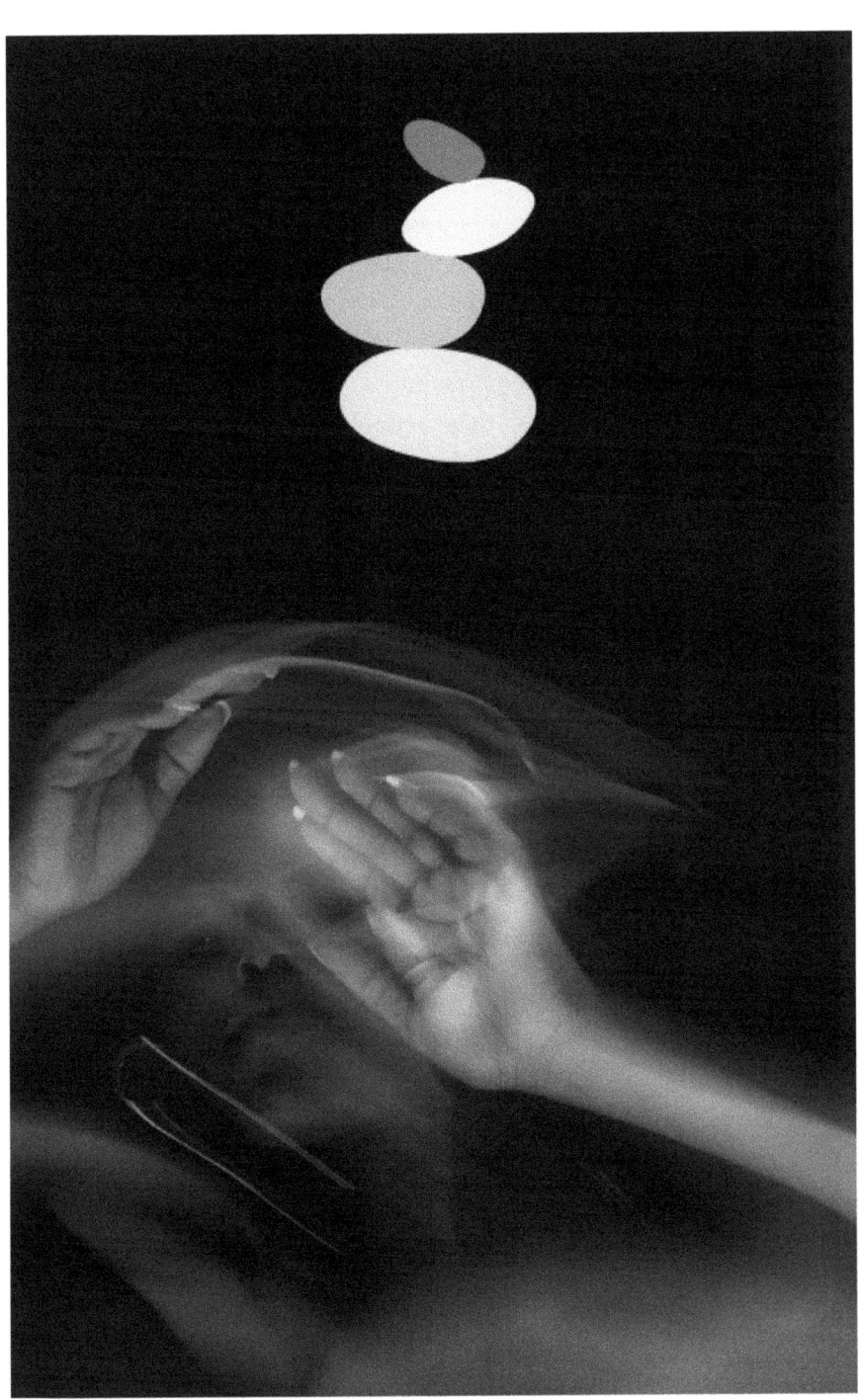

The Nature of Chaos

Chaos is an inherent aspect of life - a swirling dance of unpredictability, change, and uncertainty. Chaos can manifest in various forms - a sudden life upheaval, unexpected challenges, or a sense of disarray in our external or internal worlds. It can leave us feeling overwhelmed, disoriented, and longing for stability. However, within the chaos, there exists a hidden order - a cosmic intelligence that guides us towards greater understanding and equilibrium.

Embracing Change and Uncertainty

Change is the catalyst that propels us towards growth and transformation. Uncertainty invites us to release our attachment to outcomes and to cultivate a deep trust in the unfolding of the journey. Embracing change and uncertainty requires a shift in perspective - a willingness to let go of the need for control and to surrender to the flow of life. We develop resilience, adaptability, and a sense of adventure as we navigate the ever-changing landscape of our lives. By embracing change, we open ourselves to the limitless possibilities that arise from the chaos.

Cultivating Inner Stability

Within the chaos, we can find a sense of inner stability - a grounded presence that remains steady amidst the turbulent currents. Cultivating inner stability involves nurturing a strong foundation within ourselves. We engage in practices such as meditation, breath work, or grounding exercises that help us connect with the present moment and anchor our awareness in the here and now. We cultivate self-care routines, prioritize our well-being, and establish healthy boundaries to maintain our inner equilibrium.

Seeking Harmony and Integration

Harmony and integration play a vital role in finding balance within chaos. We recognize that balance is not about suppressing or avoiding chaos but about finding a harmonious relationship with it. Seeking harmony involves finding a sense of alignment within ourselves - the

integration of our thoughts, emotions, and actions. We engage in practices that promote self-reflection, self-awareness,
and the cultivation of inner harmony. By embracing the wholeness of our being, we navigate the chaos with a greater sense of clarity and ease. Integration involves weaving the diverse aspects of our lives into a cohesive whole.

We explore the interconnectedness of our relationships, work, passions, and personal well-being. We recognize that finding balance within chaos is not about compartmentalization but about embracing the interplay of all aspects of our existence.

Embracing Flexibility and Adaptability

Flexibility and adaptability are essential qualities in finding balance within chaos. We recognize that rigidity and resistance only contribute to further imbalance, while flexibility and adaptability allow us to flow with the ever-changing nature of life. Embracing flexibility involves being open to new perspectives, ideas, and possibilities. We release attachments to fixed outcomes and embrace the beauty of unexpected turns and detours. By embracing flexibility, we cultivate a greater sense of ease, resilience, and a willingness to embrace the lessons and growth that emerge from the chaos. Adaptability is the art of adjusting and responding to changing circumstances. We develop a nimble mindset, allowing us to navigate the twists and turns of the chaotic journey. We cultivate a willingness to learn, unlearn, and reframe our perceptions in light of new information or experiences. Through adaptability, we find balance within the ever-shifting currents of chaos.

In conclusion, finding balance within chaos is a transformative journey that invites us to embrace change, uncertainty, and the inherent unpredictability of life. By cultivating inner stability, seeking harmony and integration, and embracing flexibility and adaptability, we navigate the chaos with grace and wisdom. May you embark on this journey with an open heart and a willingness to embrace the transformative power of finding balance within chaos. Embrace the ever-changing nature of life, for within the chaos lies the potential for growth, clarity, and profound self-discovery.

Chapter 5
Tools for Clarity

The Power of Self-Reflection

Self-reflection is a powerful tool for gaining clarity and self-understanding. Self-reflection invites us to turn our gaze inward and examine our thoughts, emotions, and behaviours. It involves creating intentional space for introspection, where we can explore our values, beliefs, and aspirations. Through practices such as journaling, meditation, or contemplative walks in nature, we engage in a process of self-inquiry that uncovers hidden truths and fosters a deeper sense of clarity.

Cultivating Mindfulness

Mindfulness is a tool that allows us to anchor our awareness in the present moment. Cultivating mindfulness involves paying attention to our thoughts, feelings, and sensations without judgment or attachment. It involves bringing a curious and non-reactive awareness to our experiences. Through practices such as mindfulness meditation, breath work, or mindful movement, we develop a greater capacity to observe our inner landscape, resulting in increased clarity and self-understanding.

The Power of Intuition

Intuition is a powerful tool for accessing deep wisdom and clarity. In this section, we explore the significance of tapping into our intuition as a means to gain clarity in our lives. We delve into practices that facilitate the development and cultivation of our intuitive abilities. Tapping into our intuition involves quieting the noise of the mind and listening to the subtle whispers of our inner guidance. It requires trust and surrender to the wisdom that arises from within. Through practices such as meditation, contemplation, or creative expression, we develop a stronger connection with our intuition, allowing it to guide us towards greater clarity and aligned decision-making.

Seeking Guidance and Support

Seeking guidance and support from trusted sources is a valuable tool for gaining clarity. We recognize the power of collaboration, mentorship, and community in supporting our quest for clarity. Seeking guidance and support involves reaching out to mentors, coaches, therapists, or wise individuals who can offer insights and perspectives beyond our own. It involves actively seeking out communities and networks that resonate with our values and aspirations. By

engaging in meaningful conversations, receiving feedback, and sharing experiences, we gain valuable insights that contribute to our clarity and growth.

Embracing Solitude and Stillness

Solitude and stillness are powerful tools for creating the space needed to cultivate clarity. Embracing solitude involves intentionally creating moments of aloneness, away from external distractions. It allows us to disconnect from the noise of the world and connect with our inner selves. Through practices such as meditation, spending time in nature, or engaging in creative pursuits, we cultivate stillness, inviting clarity to emerge from the depths of our being.

Cultivating Discernment

Cultivating discernment is a tool that empowers us to make choices aligned with our values and aspirations. Cultivating discernment involves developing the capacity to differentiate between what serves our growth and what hinders it. It involves tuning into our inner compass and aligning our choices with our deepest values and aspirations. Through practices such as self-inquiry, reflection on consequences, or seeking different perspectives, we refine our discernment and make decisions that lead to greater clarity and alignment.

In conclusion, tools for clarity empower us to navigate the journey of self-discovery with greater insight, wisdom, and self-understanding. By engaging in self-reflection, cultivating mindfulness, tapping into our intuition, seeking guidance, embracing solitude and stillness, and cultivating discernment, we access the transformative power of clarity in our lives. May you embrace these tools with openness and curiosity, knowing that they are catalysts for profound self-discovery and aligned action. Embrace the power of clarity, for it guides you towards a life lived with purpose, authenticity, and deep fulfilment.

Chapter 6
Transcending Limitations

The Nature of Limitations

Limitations are beliefs, fears, and patterns that hold us back from realizing our full potential. Limitations often stem from conditioning, societal norms, past experiences, and self-imposed beliefs. They create boundaries that confine our perception of what is possible. However, by recognizing and challenging these limitations, we embark on a journey of self-discovery and growth, transcending the boundaries that restrict our potential.

Uncovering Limiting Beliefs

Limiting beliefs are deeply ingrained ideas about ourselves, others, and the world that limit our self-perception and potential. They often arise from past experiences, societal conditioning, or negative self-talk. By engaging in self-inquiry, journaling, or working with a therapist or coach, we uncover and challenge these limiting beliefs, creating space for new perspectives and possibilities.

Cultivating Self-Compassion and Empowerment

Cultivating self-compassion and empowerment is an essential aspect of transcending limitations. Self-compassion involves extending kindness and understanding towards ourselves as we navigate the process of transcending limitations. It requires us to embrace our vulnerabilities and imperfections with love and acceptance. Through practices such as self-care, self-reflection, and positive affirmations, we cultivate a nurturing and supportive relationship with ourselves, fostering the courage to step beyond our perceived limitations.

Empowerment is the process of recognizing and accessing our inner strength and capabilities. It involves shifting our focus from what we lack to what we have to offer. By honouring our unique gifts, talents, and strengths, we gain confidence and resilience to transcend limitations. Through practices such as visualization, affirmations, or engaging in empowering activities, we cultivate a sense of personal agency and liberation.

Embracing Growth Mindset

Embracing a growth mindset is a powerful tool for transcending limitations.

A growth mindset is the belief that our abilities, intelligence, and skills can be developed through effort, perseverance, and a willingness to learn. It involves embracing challenges, seeing setbacks as opportunities for growth, and

believing in our capacity for continuous improvement. By shifting our perspective from fixed limitations to expansive possibilities, we open ourselves to new experiences, knowledge, and personal evolution.

Stepping into the Unknown

Stepping into the unknown is a transformative act that allows us to transcend limitations. Stepping into the unknown involves taking risks, embracing uncertainty, and venturing beyond familiar territory. It requires us to release the need for control and security, allowing the uncharted path to reveal new insights and possibilities. By engaging in practices such as exploring new interests, trying new experiences, or embarking on new adventures, we expand our horizons and transcend the limitations that once held us back.

Cultivating Resilience and Perseverance

Cultivating resilience and perseverance is essential for transcending limitations.

Resilience is the ability to bounce back from adversity and setbacks. It involves developing emotional strength, adaptability, and a belief in our capacity to overcome obstacles. By engaging in practices that enhance resilience, such as self-care, self-reflection, and seeking support, we cultivate the inner fortitude to persist and rise above limitations. Perseverance is the commitment to staying the course despite challenges and setbacks. It involves maintaining focus, determination, and a belief in the value of our aspirations. By developing a growth mindset, setting clear goals, and celebrating progress, we cultivate perseverance and the resilience needed to transcend limitations.

In conclusion, transcending limitations is a transformative journey that empowers us to break free from self-imposed boundaries and expand our potential. By uncovering limiting beliefs, cultivating self-compassion and empowerment, embracing a growth mindset, stepping into the unknown, and cultivating resilience and perseverance, we transcend the limitations that once held us back. May you embrace this journey with courage and determination, knowing that the path to self-realization lies beyond the boundaries of perceived limitations. Embrace the transformative power of transcending limitations, for it leads to personal growth, self-discovery, and the realization of your fullest potential.

Chapter 7
Uniting Spirit and Mind

The Duality of Spirit and Mind

Spirit and mind represent two essential aspects of our being - the transcendent and the immanent, the intuitive and the analytical. Spirit represents our connection to the divine, the intuitive wisdom that resides within us. Mind represents our intellectual capacity, analytical thinking, and rationality. These two aspects often seem to be in conflict, but by recognizing their complementary nature, we can harmonize them and tap into their synergistic potential.

Embracing Intuition and Intellect

Embracing intuition involves connecting with our inner wisdom, listening to the subtle whispers of our soul, and trusting our intuitive guidance. By engaging in practices such as meditation, mindfulness, or creative expression, we nurture our intuitive capacities, allowing them to inform and enrich our decision-making process. Embracing intellect involves utilizing our analytical and rational thinking to discern, analyse, and make sense of the world around us. By engaging in critical thinking, research, and logical reasoning, we develop a deeper understanding of ourselves and the world, complementing the intuitive insights that arise from our spiritual connection.

Cultivating Mindfulness and Presence

Cultivating mindfulness and presence is a powerful tool for uniting spirit and mind. Mindfulness involves bringing our attention to the present moment, cultivating a non-judgmental awareness of our thoughts, emotions, and sensations. By practising mindfulness meditation, conscious breathing, or engaging in mindful activities, we anchor our awareness in the here and now, fostering a sense of presence that unites spirit and mind. Presence is a state of deep connection with the present moment and the essence of our being. It involves fully engaging with our experiences, free from the distractions of the past or future. Through practices such as meditation, embodiment practices, or spending time in nature, we cultivate a state of presence that allows the integration of spirit and mind, leading to greater clarity and alignment.

Balancing Logic and Intuition

Balancing logic and intuition is a key aspect of uniting spirit and mind. Logic and reason provide us with structure, analysis, and a systematic approach to understanding the world. Intuition, on the other hand, offers us insights, creativity, and a direct connection to our higher wisdom. By honouring and integrating both modes of knowing, we access a more comprehensive and holistic understanding of ourselves and the world around us. Finding the balance involves recognizing when to engage our analytical mind and when to tap into our intuitive wisdom. It requires us to discern which mode of knowing is most appropriate in different situations. By combining the strengths of both logic and intuition, we access a synergistic intelligence that guides us towards greater clarity and alignment.

Embodying Spiritual Values in Daily Life

Embodying spiritual values in daily life is a powerful way to unite spirit and mind. Uniting spirit and mind involves living from a place of alignment with our highest values, principles, and aspirations. It requires us to bridge the gap between our spiritual insights and the practical aspects of our daily lives. By embodying qualities such as compassion, kindness, integrity, and gratitude, we bring the transcendent aspects of our being into the immanent realm of our everyday experiences. Through conscious choices, mindful actions, and intentional living, we align our thoughts, words, and deeds with our spiritual essence. By integrating our spiritual values into our relationships, work, and contributions to the world, we create a harmonious and purposeful existence that unites spirit and mind.

In conclusion, uniting spirit and mind is a transformative journey that invites us to embrace the duality within ourselves and cultivate a harmonious integration of these aspects. By embracing intuition and intellect, cultivating mindfulness and presence, balancing logic and intuition, and embodying spiritual values in daily life, we bridge the gap between the transcendent and the immanent, leading to a state of wholeness and alignment. May you embark on this journey with openness and curiosity, knowing that the union of spirit and mind holds the key to profound self-discovery, wisdom, and a life lived with purpose and authenticity. Embrace the transformative power of uniting spirit and mind, for it leads to a profound sense of wholeness, clarity, and connection with your true essence.

Chapter 8
Embracing the Journey

The Beauty of the Journey

The journey of life is a tapestry of experiences, lessons, and growth opportunities. The beauty of the journey lies in its unpredictability and the myriad of experiences it offers. It is in the twists and turns, the challenges and triumphs, that we discover our strength, resilience, and capacity for growth. By embracing the journey, we release the need for control and surrender to the flow of life, opening ourselves to the vast possibilities that await.

Cultivating Presence and Gratitude

Cultivating presence and gratitude is a powerful tool for embracing the journey.

Presence involves bringing our attention to the here and now, fully immersing ourselves in the present moment. By engaging in practices such as mindfulness, meditation, or conscious breathing, we anchor ourselves in the richness of each experience, savouring the beauty and lessons it holds. Gratitude is the practice of recognizing and appreciating the blessings, opportunities, and lessons that the journey presents to us. By cultivating a grateful mindset, we shift our focus from what is lacking to the abundance that surrounds us. Through gratitude journaling, acts of kindness, or simply pausing to acknowledge the gifts of each day, we open our hearts to the transformative power of gratitude.

Embracing Change and Uncertainty

Embracing change and uncertainty is an essential aspect of fully embracing the journey. We recognize that within these shifts and unknowns lie opportunities for growth, self-discovery, and the unfolding of our true potential. Change is a constant companion on the journey, propelling us forward and inviting us to evolve. By embracing change, we release resistance and open ourselves to the transformative power it holds. We learn to adapt, let go of what no longer serves us, and welcome the new beginnings that arise. Uncertainty is an inherent aspect of the journey, challenging us to trust the unknown and have faith in the unfolding of our path. By embracing uncertainty, we develop resilience, courage, and a willingness to explore new territories. We learn to navigate the uncharted waters with curiosity and an open heart, knowing that within the uncertainty lies the potential for profound self-discovery and growth.

Embracing the Lessons

Embracing the lessons that the journey presents is a transformative act. Every

experience, whether joyful or challenging, carries valuable lessons and insights. By embracing the lessons, we honour the growth opportunities that the journey offers. We cultivate a sense of curiosity, self-reflection, and a willingness to learn from both our successes and setbacks. Through journaling, contemplation, or seeking the wisdom of mentors or teachers, we integrate the lessons into our being, allowing them to shape and guide our path.

Trusting the Process

Trusting the process is a key element in embracing the journey. We recognize that the journey is a personal and unique experience, and by trusting the process, we allow our highest potential to unfold. Trusting the process involves surrendering to the divine intelligence that guides our journey. It requires us to release the need for immediate answers or fixed outcomes and to have faith in the timing and synchronicity of life. By developing a deep trust in ourselves, the universe, and the innate wisdom that resides within, we navigate the journey with grace and a sense of alignment.

In conclusion, embracing the journey is a transformative act that invites us to fully engage with the present moment and the profound wisdom that arises from each experience. By cultivating presence and gratitude, embracing change and uncertainty, embracing the lessons, and trusting the process, we embark on a journey of self-discovery, growth, and the realization of our highest potential. May you embrace the journey with an open heart and a sense of wonder, knowing that within the unfolding lies the transformative power that leads to profound self-understanding, fulfilment, and a life lived with purpose and authenticity. Embrace the beauty of the journey, for it is in embracing the journey that we truly come alive.

Conclusion

SPIRITUAL PSYCHOSIS: A GUIDE TO SPIRITUAL PSYCHOSIS FOR FINDING CLARITY

In this journey through the realms of spiritual psychosis, we have delved into the depths of the human experience, exploring the complexities, challenges, and transformative potential that arise on the path to finding clarity. Throughout the chapters of this book, we have explored the calling of the soul, unveiled the shadows, dived into the inner alchemy, found balance in chaos, discovered tools for clarity, united spirit and mind, and embraced the journey itself. Now, as we reach the conclusion of this guide, we invite you to reflect on the transformative insights gained and take a moment to consider the impact this journey can have on your life.

The path of spiritual psychosis is not an easy one. It tests our resolve, challenges our beliefs, and confronts us with the unknown. It requires us to face our fears, embrace our shadows, and navigate the paradoxes that arise. But within this intricate tapestry of experiences lies the potential for profound growth, clarity, and liberation. It is through traversing the depths of our being that we uncover the wisdom that lies within, enabling us to navigate the complexities of life with newfound clarity and purpose.

We have explored the importance of self-awareness, introspection, and integration in cultivating clarity amidst the challenges of spiritual imbalance. We have delved into the power of grounding techniques, meditation, journaling, and various modalities that aid in finding balance and connecting with our true selves. We have emphasized the significance of transcending limitations, uniting spirit and mind, and embracing the journey with openness and curiosity. Each chapter has been a stepping stone towards greater clarity and a deeper understanding of our own spiritual growth.

As the author of this book, I humbly invite you to review and share your experience of reading this guide. Your reviews not only serve as a valuable feedback for me as an author but also act as a guide for other readers who may be seeking clarity and transformation in their own lives. By sharing your thoughts, insights, and the impact this book has had on you, you contribute to a collective ripple effect, allowing more readers to find solace, guidance, and support in their own spiritual journeys.

It is my hope that this guide has served as a companion on your path, offering insights, tools, and perspectives that have ignited a spark of clarity within you. May it empower you to embrace the challenges that arise, honour your unique journey, and seek the profound wisdom that resides within your own being. As you continue your exploration of the spiritual realms, remember that the path to

clarity is not a destination but an ongoing journey of self-discovery, growth, and transformation.

I extend my deepest gratitude to you for embarking on this journey with me. Your presence and willingness to delve into the depths of spiritual psychosis have made this guide come alive. May you carry the wisdom gained from these pages into your everyday life, enriching your relationships, deepening your connection with the divine, and finding clarity amidst the tapestry of existence.

With heartfelt appreciation, I invite you to review this book and share your experience with others. Together, let us create a ripple effect of transformation and guide more seekers towards the path of clarity, purpose, and self-discovery. Thank you.

In clarity and unity,

Dr. Jilesh

www.ingramcontent.com/pod-product-compliance
Ingram Content Group UK Ltd.
Pitfield, Milton Keynes, MK11 3LW, UK
UKHW022217230426
12048UKWH00016BA/901